Osborne

Michael Turner

D0316578

Introduction

Queen Victoria and Prince Albert bought the Osborne estate on the Isle of Wight in 1845. Here they built a new private home as an escape from court life in London and Windsor. Its Italianate design became known as 'the Osborne style' and was imitated throughout the British empire. The rooms are filled with furniture and works of art that mirror the couple's personal tastes; the planting in the grounds is to Albert's designs. The most private rooms can be visited, including the nursery and Queen Victoria's bedroom, where she died.

Queen Victoria used Osborne for more than 50 years, and entertained visiting ministers, foreign royalty, and her own extensive family here. A large and efficient household was needed to ensure that all arrangements ran smoothly, and part of the basement service rooms are on display. Members of the household who were especially influential were the queen's Highland servant John Brown, who came here from Balmoral in 1864, Henry Ponsonby, her private secretary from 1870 to 1895, and Abdul Karim, her Indian secretary during the 1880s.

After Prince Albert's death in 1861, Queen Victoria found solace at Osborne. While she aimed to be guided in everything by what Albert would have wished, changes were made, notably the building of the Durbar Room in the 1890s, with its extraordinary Indian interior and collection of Indian artefacts, which compliments the queen's title of 'empress of India'.

Queen Victoria died in 1901 and the house was opened to the public in 1904. Part of the building was converted to a convalescent home, and there was a Royal Naval College in the grounds. These have both since closed, and more of Osborne is now open to the public than ever. Many rooms and exteriors have been recently restored by English Heritage to display the tastes of Osborne's former royal owners.

Above: *Princess Beatrice in a nautilus shell, carved in marble by Mary Thornycroft, 1858. Over a period of 15 years Thornycroft made a sculpture of each of the nine children. They can all be seen in the drawing room*

Facing page: *The Pavilion seen from the lower terrace*

Tour of Osborne

Osborne was built as a family
home by the sea rather than
a palace, and the Pavilion at the
heart of the house represents
an embodiment of Victorian family
values. Lived in for only 55 years,
the house is a unique evocation
of the private tastes and ambitions
of Victoria and Albert. It also
presents a vivid and touching
re-creation of royal daily life
at both domestic and court level.

FOLLOWING THE TOUR

*The tour takes visitors into the house via the
household wing, through the ground floor and Pavilion
basement, before returning to the ground floor. Visitors
then have the option of climbing the steep back
stairs to the second floor, before visiting the first floor
and the ground floor of the Durbar Wing, or of
retracing their steps to use the lifts. The garden tour
takes in the terraces, walled garden and ice house
before exploring the royal children's gardens and the
Swiss Cottage. If the house is crowded, it might be
more convenient to start at the Swiss Cottage.*

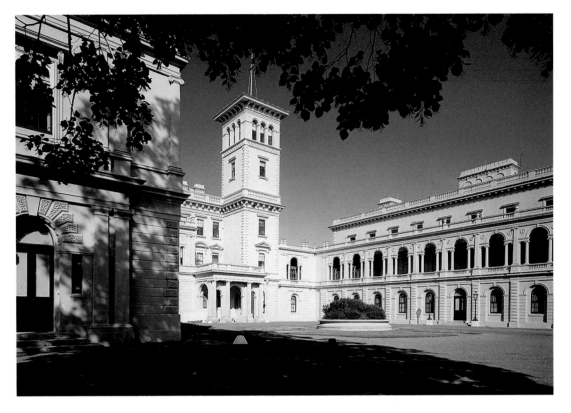

THE EXTERIOR

The household wing, the first part of the house encountered from the south, accommodated members of the royal household, offices and guests, and was completed by the London building contractor Thomas Cubitt (1788–1855) in 1851, as was the main wing to its rear. It is built of brick with a cement render coloured to look like stone. The window frames are mahogany and were painted in Queen Victoria's lifetime to protect the wood. The four cement copies of classical statues at first-floor level were commercially available, and demonstrate Prince Albert's desire to clothe Osborne with classical respectability, but at a cost to suit the queen's privy purse.

On the far right is a small attached building whose only entrance is the outside door. This is the smoking room, built in 1866 for the prince of Wales because the queen would not tolerate smoking in the house. It is not open to the public.

To the left of the household wing is the carriage ring. The iron lamps supported by dolphins are a reminder that Osborne was a seaside home.

The Grand Corridor is on the right. Above, the arcade of Ionic Venetian windows was inspired by Andrea Palladio's arcading to the basilica at Vicenza (built 1549–1614). The arcade gave access from the Pavilion to the elder children's apartments in the main wing, which overlooks the terraces and Osborne bay. A glazed passage between the pavilion and the main wing was added in 1877.

The central block is the Pavilion, the first part of Osborne built by Cubitt in 1846 to house the family's private apartments. The only extensive use of real stone on the exterior is the Portland stone porte cochère, where travellers could alight from a carriage under cover.

In 1890 John Randall Mann (1828–1918), who served his apprenticeship with Cubitt and who had been surveyor of works at Osborne since 1857, designed the Durbar Wing to the left. Unlike its interior, its façades are conservative, to blend with the Italianate style of the main house.

Visitors to the household wing would have entered up the steps, flanked by copies of the Calydonian boar on the left and the dog of Alcibiades on the right. The dog is the original cement statue, supplied by the London artificial-stone manufacturer Austin & Seeley.

An introductory exhibition is located in what was formerly the household dining room. The plaster cornice depicting grapes indicates its original function. The household wing corridor leads into the Grand Corridor.

Above: The carriage ring, with the Grand Corridor on the right and the porte cochère of the Pavilion in the centre. The cement basket in the centre was first planted with heather by Prince Albert in 1849

Below: The Calydonian boar at the entrance to the household wing. This modern stone sculpture copies the original destroyed in 1918

Facing page: Detail of the embossed wallpaper below the gallery of the Durbar Room

Above: Nymph and Cupid *by Edward Muller, commissioned as a birthday present for Albert before his death in 1861*

Below: The Marine Venus *in the Grand Corridor is from the Baths of Caracalla in Rome, and was bought at the Stowe sale of 1847*

■ GRAND CORRIDOR

The Grand Corridor forms a link between the household and main wings, and Queen Victoria's private apartments. The decoration (largely repainted in the 1980s) was devised by Prince Albert in conjunction with Ludwig Gruner, and reflects his liking for Italian Renaissance design.

High on the walls are reduced plaster copies of reliefs of friezes from the Parthenon, modelled and supplied by the sculptor John Henning (1771–1851) in 1846. The corridor was designed to resemble a classical sculpture gallery, common in late 18th- and 19th-century country houses. However, at Osborne most of the sculptures were by living British and European artists. Unlike other royal residences, Osborne was lived in for only 55 years, and so clearly demonstrates the tastes of Victoria and Albert, who were the sole builders of the collection. In many ways it is Albert's creation. After his death in 1861 the queen added to the collection but did not alter significantly the prince's arrangement of it. Her additions were perhaps less scholarly, and more sentimental in character.

The ebonized cabinets are part of the 1850s decorative scheme. The bronzes on top of them are mostly reduced copies of antique figures and popular works.

Halfway down the corridor is a statue of Queen Victoria in classical costume by John Gibson (1790–1866) in a gilded niche. The queen gave it to Albert for his birthday in 1849. In front of the statue, sections of the elaborate Minton tile floor are exposed. The design includes the arms of Great Britain and maritime symbols.

The main wing to the right housed principal guests, and the royal children when they left the nursery. The ground-floor corridor has not been restored, so the varnish on the marbled pilasters and skirtings has yellowed with age.

2 COUNCIL ROOM

The queen's privy council of ministers met in the council room several times a year. At a meeting here in June 1857 the queen gave Prince Albert the title 'prince consort'. At other times the room was used for entertaining – dancing, charades and drama. In the corridor opposite is a lift installed for the convalescent home in what was originally an alcove giving light on to the corridor, where ministers waited to attend a meeting.

The council room is the most elaborately decorated at Osborne. Gruner and Albert settled the colour scheme, which was completed in 1859. In the centre of the ceiling is the badge of the Order of the Garter and other royal emblems. As in most of the fine rooms at Osborne, the original paint survives in the picking-out of ceiling elements, whereas the larger areas of plain colour on the ceiling and walls have been over-painted.

The door through which visitors enter is flanked by portraits on Sèvres porcelain of Queen Victoria and Prince Albert which were presented by Louis Philippe, the king of France, in 1846. The painting *The Deer Drive* on the end wall is a Victorian copy of the original intended for this room by Sir Edwin Landseer (1802–73). French windows lead on to the upper terrace.

On 14 January 1878 in this room Alexander Graham Bell demonstrated his telephone, which had been patented for less than two years. 'It is rather faint and one must hold the tube rather close to one's ear,' commented the queen, but telephones were nevertheless installed in 1885.

The convalescent home used the room for smoking, hence the severe yellowing of the ceiling.

Nineteenth-century photographs show the silk chenille carpet by Templeton's of Glasgow dated MDCCCLI (1851), which was displayed in Prince Albert's Great Exhibition that year and bought by Queen Victoria, who had it adapted to fit. It remained at Osborne until the 1920s, when it went to the British embassy in Washington DC. It was subsequently deposited at the Smithsonian Institute, which generously presented the carpet to English Heritage in 1988 for redisplay.

Over the doors on each side of the marble chimneypiece are pediments containing medallions of Prince Albert and Queen Victoria supported by Roman gods and goddesses, which were added in 1855 by William Theed (1804–91), Queen Victoria's favourite sculptor. The left-hand door leads into the audience room.

Left: The council room set for a privy council meeting in about 1857. The plain ceiling and doors were elaborately redecorated in 1859

Below: The council room, showing the Templeton's carpet

❸ AUDIENCE ROOM

Queen Victoria frequently received ministers here before privy council meetings. Holland & Sons supplied the original furniture in 1851 and much of it survives, including the writing table and gilt satinwood chairs upholstered with crimson damask. The remarkable coloured glass and ormolu (gilt brass) chandelier represents convolvulus (Albert's favourite flower) and arum lilies climbing out of a basket. It was probably manufactured in Berlin.

❶ GRAND CORRIDOR (CONTINUED)

The queen took exercise here on the rare occasions when bad weather stopped her going out. The white and gold candelabra with two-burner lamps and bird's-beak benches with morocco-leather seats form part of the original furniture.

A grey marble statue on the left is of Antinous, the emperor Hadrian's favourite page, who was drowned in the Nile in AD 122. It was thought to be Egypto-Roman when it was sold at Northwood Park, Cowes, in 1850, but is now believed to be a 19th-century copy of a statue in the Vatican. The white marble statue is a winged Victory by C D Rauch (1777–1857).

The corridor turns left. Near the end is a bay window and the opposite wall contains an inset panel by John Gibson of Cupid and Psyche, who swore eternal love for each other and with whom the royal couple identified themselves.

Beyond, the main entrance hall to the Pavilion is painted in imitation of grey marble. The mahogany side table, cupboard and chairs are typical of austere early-Victorian hall furniture.

Above: The statue of Noble, Queen Victoria's collie, by Sir Joseph Edgar Boehm (1834–90)

Right: The audience room. The cabinet of c.1870 by Holland & Sons contains nine porcelain medallions of the royal children painted by Carl Schmidt. The oil painting, Christ in the Temple by Marie Ellenrieder, was bought by Prince Albert in 1849

SECOND
FLOOR

FIRST
FLOOR

GROUND
FLOOR

BASEMENT

The Pavilion

Cubitt completed the Pavilion in 1845. Inside, he was influenced by a London Georgian townhouse plan. The basement houses service rooms including a boiler room with the necessary coal cellars underneath the carriage ring (not open to the public). The principal rooms at ground-floor level envelop a spacious full-height staircase hall, but the arrangement of a suite of salons – the dining room leading into the drawing room, which in turn leads in to the billiard room – is more continental in style. It suggests the prince's German background. The couple's most intimate rooms are on the first floor, with Albert's domain on the right and the queen's on the left, both meeting in the shared sitting room. The nurseries and servants' rooms are on the second floor.
The 32.6m tall flag tower contains an observation room reached by a spiral staircase (not open to the public).

Basement Table-deckers' rooms

Ground floor Anticlockwise from grand staircase: dining room; drawing room; billiard room; horn room

First floor Anticlockwise from grand staircase: Queen Victoria's bedroom; Queen Victoria's dressing room; Queen Victoria's sitting room; Prince Albert's dressing room; Prince Albert's bathroom; pages' alcove

Second floor Anticlockwise from grand staircase: nursery sitting room and governess's bedroom; nursery bedroom

TABLE-DECKERS' ROOMS

Steep servants' stairs lead down to the Pavilion basement and the table-deckers' rooms, which are immediately beneath the dining room. The function of table-decker was unique to the royal household, and was within the department of the lord steward, who oversaw all the kitchen staff. Table-deckers were responsible for laying the dining tables for lunch and dinner and arranging displays of flowers from the kitchen garden. They also made the final preparations to the food. This came from the kitchen court, situated about 100m away to prevent cooking smells reaching the dining room. The table-deckers needed a hot closet in its own small room to keep the food warm. Their rooms also contain ample cupboards for china and lead-lined sinks in the inner room for washing glasses. The room was used only as a store after the queen's death, so the Victorian painted decoration has largely survived, including the blue-painted walls inside the glazed cupboards – blue was believed to discourage flies.

4 DINING ROOM

The dining room, drawing room and billiard room are the three principal reception rooms in the Pavilion. They are all richly decorated, and each contains an elaborate ceiling painted in 1857 to designs by Gruner and restored by English Heritage.

Carpeted stairs lead from the table-deckers' rooms to the dining room: food and plates could be brought directly up and laid out on the large mahogany sideboard. This, and the four side tables, have lion monopodia legs and were designed by Henry Whitaker in about 1847.

In the 1850s dinner was served promptly at 8pm. It had shifted to 8.45pm towards the end of the century, but it was frequently 9.15pm before the queen arrived and the company could sit down to eat. One of the dining tables shows the laying for dinner in progress, with the set square and ruler used by the table-deckers to ensure each setting was perfect. Osborne has no breakfast room, so the dining room sometimes performed that function when it was too cold for the queen to eat breakfast outside.

Family portraits have always hung in the dining room. The largest, above the sideboard, is a Victorian copy of the family group by Franz Xaver Winterhalter (1805–73) which was hung here on

Left: The drawing room in the 1870s. It was initially lit by candles in the three cut-glass chandeliers made by Osler's of Birmingham

Below: One of the pair of pedestal chandeliers by Osler's, whose design Prince Albert supervised and which were displayed at the Great Exhibition of 1851

Facing page top: Table-deckers' scullery below the dining room

Bottom: The dining room

Queen Victoria's birthday in 1849. To its left is a Victorian copy of Winterhalter's portrait of the duchess of Kent, Queen Victoria's mother.

The marriage of Princess Alice to Prince Louis of Hesse took place here in 1862. Overshadowed by the continued mourning for the prince consort, who had died the previous December, it was described by the queen as 'more like a funeral'. It was also in this room that the queen's body lay in state in 1901 before being taken to Windsor.

5 DRAWING ROOM

Queen Victoria described the drawing room in 1846 as 'extremely handsome, with its yellow damask satin curtains and furniture to match'. The room was restored in 2003 to reflect its appearance in the 1890s, with repainted walls, curtains and upholstery based on archive samples, and a copy of the intricately patterned Aubusson carpet, which was made to fit the marbled columns in the room. Full-length mirrors in heavy shutters reflected the brilliant candlelight from the three cut-glass chandeliers by Osler's of Birmingham (the current chandeliers are replicas). The pair of cut-glass pedestal chandeliers near the bay window are original and were also made by Osler's. All the chandeliers were wired for electricity in 1893.

The room was furnished more sparsely and formally until the 1870s. That it appeared formal even then is evident from a remark by Mary Bulteel, lady-in-waiting to Queen Victoria, in 1858 which also contains an insight into Prince Albert's enthusiasm for scientific theories: 'I have routed the pianoforte out from the wall, to sit with one's face towards the people, instead of one's back; put the sofa crooked, with the round table near it, instead of stiffly in the middle of the room; the armchair crookedly and comfortably near the fire. If P.A. [Prince Albert] says anything about the pianoforte I shall stop his mouth with a little bit of scientific theory about the properties stone walls have of absorbing sound.'

This room contains some idealised statues of Queen Victoria's children which were carved by Mary Thornycroft from 1845 to 1860, with a mixture of family portraits and landscapes.

Visiting foreign royalty were received in this room, and the queen generally retired here after dinner to play cards or to sing and play at the Erard piano with members of the household. Both the piano and six cabinets surmounting the bookcases are decorated with porcelain plaques painted by Carl Schmidt showing miniature copies of Italian Old Master paintings. Celebrated

musicians also gave recitals here, including the soprano Jenny Lind (1820–87), known as the 'Swedish nightingale', who appeared at Osborne in 1847 (three months after her London debut) with Luigi Lablache, the celebrated bass singer, from whom the queen had singing lessons.

6 BILLIARD ROOM

The right-angled plan of the billiard room, with its columned screen and drawn curtains, could hide it from the adjacent drawing room. This meant that the men could play billiards after dinner and sit on the raised bench while the queen remained in the next room. Technically, the men were still within the queen's presence, and protocol required them to stand unless given permission to sit.

The slate billiard table was manufactured by Magnus. The legs were enamelled to represent marble, and the frieze panels were designed by Prince Albert, as was the elaborate light fitting. It was converted to electricity in 1893 (the original bank of brass light switches for this room with wiring hidden behind timber 'capping and casing' survives to the right of the door). The queen learnt to play billiards while at Osborne, and her journal records games with the women of the household after lunch.

Above the bench is *Cardinal Wolsey at the Gate of Leicester Abbey*.

A door leads to the principal stairwell, the walls of which were painted by the 'decorative artist' Anthony Muller in 1861 (who also worked at Buckingham Palace). William Theed's posthumous bust of the prince consort sits on a marble base, which houses a ventilator – part of Cubitt's heating system, which was controlled by a coal-fired boiler in the basement. The steep servants' back stairs have a simple handrail and iron balusters, and gave access to all the upper floors.

Above: The billiard room. George Magnus made both the billiard table and the cue stand by the end wall. His works were near Cubitt's yard in Pimlico, London, and the table was probably transported to Osborne on one of Cubitt's barges

Left: Cardinal Wolsey at the Gate of Leicester Abbey, commissioned for the billiard room in 1847 by Prince Albert from Charles West Cope (1811–90)

Facing page: The drawing room, restored in 2003 to reflect its appearance in the 1890s, with replica soft-furnishings, including the Aubusson carpet, and electrified chandeliers

Above: One of the many
babies' limbs, which the
queen had sculpted in marble
Right: Pen drawing by Prince
Albert of the princess royal
and the prince of Wales, 1843
Below: The nursery bedroom,
re-created as it was in
a photograph of 1873

NURSERY

The nursery suite gives an insight into Queen
Victoria and Prince Albert's relations with their
young family. It was sited immediately above the
couple's private apartments to allow them easy
access to the children, who normally remained
there until the age of six.

The first and second rooms originally formed
the sitting room and bedroom of Lady Lyttelton,
the superintendent of the royal children until
1851. Her role in overseeing the wellbeing of the
children was wide-ranging; she described some of
her duties in 1849: 'Accounts, tradesmen's letters,
maids' quarrels, bad fitting of frocks, desirableness
of rhubarb and magnesia, and, by way of
intellectual pursuits, false French genders and
elements of the multiplication table'.

Folding doors originally divided the two
rooms, but these were removed during alterations
in 1903 to accommodate the house governor of

the convalescent home. The wallpaper has not
survived, so English Heritage repainted both
rooms to match the aqua-green 'builder's finish'
found elsewhere in the house.

7 Nursery Sitting Room

The first room in the 1890s became the schoolroom for the children of Prince and Princess Henry of Battenberg. It has been restored as the nursery sitting room, and contains framed photographs that show how the present royal families of Europe, both reigning and exiled, are descended from Queen Victoria. The queen and Prince Albert had nine children and made ambitious plans for their marriages. They looked to the European royal families for suitable partners, to create a network of diplomatic and royal connections that they hoped would help secure peace and stability in Europe. However, the Prussian-Danish conflict of 1863 and the Prussian-Austrian war of 1866 made the queen realise that the policy of cementing foreign alliances by marriage was no longer capable of halting European wars. This fact was even more tragically underlined when the First World War broke out in 1914 between Germany, led by her grandson, Kaiser Wilhelm II, and Britain. However, it is through those marriages that the present reigning monarchs of Britain, Spain, Norway, Denmark and Sweden trace their ancestry to Queen Victoria.

the washstand when he was 17. Below it hangs a copy of a sketch by Queen Victoria of Eos, his favourite greyhound.

In the 1890s a member of the household commented, 'All round the room are literally stacks of toys.' Almost all that remain are Princess Louise's wicker trug and Princess Helena's exercise clubs. The doll's house is a copy of a mid-19th-century German original in the photograph.

The remaining rooms on this floor were used as maids' bedrooms and the nursery kitchen.

Above: A 19th-century German musical box. The figures move to music from Tannhäuser, *by Richard Wagner (1813–83)*
Below: Painting in the nursery bedroom by J Lucas of Prince Albert, Princess Victoria and Eos, his favourite greyhound from Coburg (1843)

8 Nursery Bedroom

The third room, the nursery bedroom, was often visited by the couple. It has been restored to match its appearance in a photograph taken in about 1873 by Jabez Hughes, a commercial photographer from Ryde, Isle of Wight, who recorded many of the buildings and interiors on the Osborne estate for Queen Victoria. By this date it was used on visits by the queen's grandchildren. None of the original decoration survived and the wallpaper, carpet and curtains are all modern. The swing cot with its mahogany frame was made for Vicky, the princess royal, in 1840. The cots, two of which are reproductions, have hinged cane-work sides and upholstered pads to protect the children. The screen shielded them from draughts, and a nurse slept in the bed. Several high chairs were used, similar to the one on display, which has an adjustable foot rail.

Many of the paintings, most of which originally hung here, had special associations for the queen and her family. Above the cots hangs a portrait of the prince consort. Albert painted the owl above

Right: The allegorical fresco Neptune Resigning the Empire of the Seas to Britannia *demonstrated Britain's supremacy as a world power. Neptune, in a shell chariot drawn by three seahorses, hands his crown via Mercury (messenger to the gods) to Britannia, who already holds Neptune's trident. Beside her is the lion of England. The figures behind her represent industry, trade and navigation*

Below: The pages' alcove. Redecorated to its original scheme in 2005, it contains modern copies of the bells that summoned the pages

9 STAIRCASE

The grand staircase was modelled on that at Claremont House, Surrey, which belonged to the queen's uncle Leopold (1790–1865), who became king of the Belgians in 1831. The walls were painted by Anthony Muller. At the head of the stairs is a life-size statue of the prince in classical armour, commissioned by him from the German sculptor Emil Wolf (1802–79) as a birthday present to the queen in 1842. It was not completed until 1844. Albert considered its 'bare legs & feet, looked too undressed to place in a room' so in 1849 a suitably shod copy was made for Buckingham Palace. Profiles in marble of Frederick and Victoria (the queen's eldest daughter), the crown prince and princess of Prussia, are inserted into the over-doors to left and right. The left-hand door originally led to the nursery kitchen, while that to the right is a plaster dummy for the sake of symmetry.

Also at the head of the stairs is the large fresco *Neptune Resigning the Empire of the Seas to Britannia* by William Dyce (1806–64), who came to Osborne in 1847 to paint it. Lady Lyttelton, whose apartments were next to it, probably saw more of him than most. She was not impressed, calling him, 'one of the least agreeable, and most dry and half-sneering mannered men I have ever met'.

10 PAGES' ALCOVE

The pages' alcove is off the first-floor landing. A page of the back stairs was in attendance at the door of the queen's apartment from 8am until she retired at night. Some of Prince Albert's early Renaissance pictures were hung here, including three by Cranach the Elder (1472–1553), but the alcove now includes a display of items belonging to George Waite (1834–1902), who was a page to Queen Victoria for more than 50 years.

The porcelain medallions bearing various Christian and classical designs are by the Danish sculptor Albert Bertel Thorvaldsen (1770–1844). The Royal Danish Porcelain Manufactory produced them in the 1840s and they are another example of the high-quality but commercially available pieces the prince chose.

The first floor was symmetrically planned about the east-west axis of the Pavilion to accommodate the private apartments of Queen Victoria and Prince Albert. The room to the left was intended to be the prince's bedroom (not open to the public). It was little, if ever, used by him and by the 1870s had become a schoolroom. Beyond are his bathroom and his dressing and writing room. In the centre is the sitting room, while the rooms on the right comprised the queen's domain: her dressing room and bedroom.

🔟 PRINCE ALBERT'S BATHROOM

The bathroom contains a plumbed-in bath, lavatory and shower – unusual in the mid-19th century. A large fresco of 1830 by A von Gegenbauer depicts Hercules laying aside his power and becoming a slave to Omphale, queen of Lydia, possibly suggesting Albert's attitude to Victoria. On the walls are some paintings by the couple and photographs of tableaux enacted by the children.

🔢 PRINCE ALBERT'S DRESSING AND WRITING ROOM

The dual function of this room is indicated by its contents: a dwarf wardrobe, washstand, and writing table. In the 19th century the walls were hung with his most precious early Renaissance pictures, almost exclusively religious. They included works by Mantegna, Bellini and Fra Angelico, some of which are now in the National Gallery in London. Above the chimney-glass is a double portrait of Albert and his brother Ernest by Louise von Meyern-Hohenburg of 1841. Queen Victoria bought it two years after her marriage.

Prince Albert's bathroom and dressing room were kept by the widowed queen as far as possible as they were during his life. She frequently used his dressing room for private, informal audiences. Randall Davidson, her chaplain from 1883 to 1891, was received by her many times in the prince's dressing room. He observed, 'Hot water was actually brought to his dressing room at dressing-time 40 years after his death . . . I have again and again had talks to her there before dinner with the hot water actually steaming.' Davidson believed the practice continued because at first the queen ordered that nothing was to be changed until she gave further instructions. The servants could not bring themselves to challenge those instructions, and as the years passed there was nothing to lead her to give contrary orders.

Second floor

First floor

Above: Painting by Queen Victoria entitled Closing Scene from 'Der Hahnenschlag'. *In 1852, the children enacted this German play by A F F von Kotzbue at Windsor Castle. In the foreground are Princesses Louise and Helena in costume*
Left: Prince Albert's dressing and writing room, where he would read or write in his 'golden morning hour' before the queen was up

17

13 QUEEN VICTORIA'S SITTING ROOM

This room is in the centre of the first floor of the Pavilion, with commanding views from the bow window across the terraces and parkland to the Solent. During the day the couple worked on the dispatch-boxes here, which constantly arrived from London via the queen's messengers. The queen sat at the left-hand desk. The three mid-19th-century bell pulls were connected to an early electric battery powered by chemical action. The bells would have summoned Miss Skerrett (the queen's principal dresser and confidante), a page, and Rudolf Löhlein, who was a Coburger and personal attendant to the prince, and later to the queen. The prince's desk to the right is identical, except that the drawers are shallower to allow for his longer legs. The prince worked here while submitting memoranda for the queen's inspection in his capacity as her private and personal secretary.

'When I am not particularly occupied,' wrote the queen in 1846, 'Vicky and Bertie alternately always take their supper in our room. Then little Helena is brought down for a quarter of an hour, followed by Affie, and then Alice.' The queen and prince could also withdraw to this room informally after dinner, either alone or with close friends. If alone, the couple might occupy themselves by pasting prints, woodcuts or sketches of places they had visited into albums, or by discussing one of Albert's projects, such as his photographic record of the complete works of Raphael. Queen Victoria's journal includes references to watching the moonlight shining on the Solent from the balcony, and listening to the nightingales in the trees below. A contemporary recorded that the queen's rooms always smelt of orange flower.

Behind the sofa is *The Good Samaritan* by Sir Charles Eastlake (1793–1865), who was keeper of the National Gallery from 1843 to 1847. After the death of the prince consort Queen Victoria accumulated the memorabilia which fill the room and include many portraits, photographs and busts of her family, including the plaster statuette by Boehm of the queen spinning with a collie at her feet, made in 1869. The actual spinning wheel nearby was made on the Athole estate in Scotland by John McGlashan aged 70 and was given to the queen by the dowager duchess of Athole in 1866.

Facing page: Queen Victoria's sitting room with her desk and Albert's side by side beneath a large ormolu (gilt brass) lamp made to burn viscous colza (vegetable) oil, gravity-fed from the raised reservoir

🄔 QUEEN VICTORIA'S DRESSING ROOM

This room contains a bath which, following contemporary propriety, looks like a wardrobe with full-length mirrors when not in use. Next to it is a shower, equally well disguised. To the left, a narrow passage contains the queen's lavatory. Access to it from the queen's bedroom was cleverly disguised to look like part of a large mahogany wardrobe.

🄕 QUEEN VICTORIA'S BEDROOM

The pattern of the printed cotton of the bed hangings, sofa and curtains incorporates profiles of the couple, and was designed for the Royal Yacht *Victoria and Albert* in the 1850s. Its use in this room is modern. *The Entombment* by Gustav Jäger (1808–71) above the chimneypiece was commissioned by Prince Albert in 1845. His fascination with gadgets is demonstrated by the

Above: Portrait of Annie Macdonald, one of a pair by Queen Victoria of the children of a Balmoral gillie, painted in 1852, the year Prince Albert acquired the Balmoral estate.

Right: Queen Victoria's dressing table, with the fine Minton porcelain dressing-table set commissioned by Prince Albert as a Christmas present in 1853

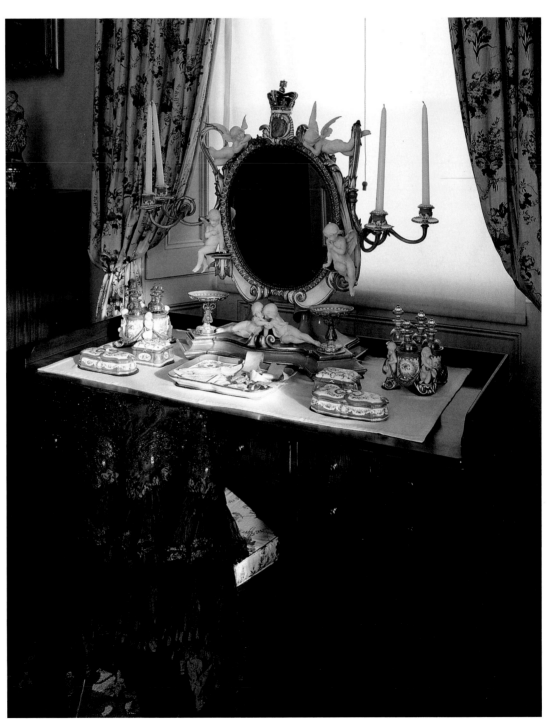

brass device that allowed the door to be bolted and unbolted from the bed. A pocket for the prince's watch is fixed to the headboard, next to a posthumous portrait of him which the widowed queen displayed in each residence.

On 22 January 1901 Queen Victoria died in this room on a small couch bed, surrounded by her children. For the next 50 years, the bedroom was set up as a family shrine, with a bronze memorial plaque on the headboard, the blinds pulled down, and an 'altar' constructed from a plans chest draped with a cloth and supporting a cross and candlesticks. In 1955 these most intimate apartments were opened to the public by permission of Queen Elizabeth II.

Outside the bedroom is an iron gate. Edward VII erected this, and the gate in the opposite corridor, after Queen Victoria's death to prevent access to these rooms which, as a general rule, were opened only to members of the royal family.

Left: Queen Victoria's bedroom, showing the bronze plaque in her memory, designed by Queen Alexandra
Below: A hand-coloured photograph of the bedroom from the 1850s. Some photographs were coloured by the queen and others by professional artists

Birthdays at Osborne

After dressing in a new summer frock, the queen was greeted at the foot of the stairs by all her children carrying nosegays

From 1848 until Albert's death, Queen Victoria was nearly always at Osborne for her birthday on 24 May. The day started at 7am with a band playing below her bedroom window – often the tune was one of Prince Albert's hymns. After dressing in a new summer frock and giving Albert one or two presents, the queen was greeted at the foot of the stairs by all her children carrying nosegays. As in her childhood, a birthday table was set out in a room decorated with flowers. In 1848 and 1849, the horn room was used, but by the 1850s a spare bedroom in the main wing became established as the 'present room'. Breakfast followed in the dining room, sometimes with the band continuing to play on the terrace. The day often concluded after dinner with dancing in the council room.

Prince Albert was almost invariably at Osborne for his birthday on 26 August. In 1851 the children sang outside his dressing room before escorting him to the present room. There followed a French play acted by the five eldest children, and as a treat the four eldest sat with their parents at the dinner table that evening for the first time. Throughout the 19th century a 'rustic fête' was also held for the estate workers in honour of the prince's birthday. It included a band, dinner in a marquee, and games such as sack races, climbing a greasy pole for a leg of mutton, and bobbing for oranges.

Children's birthdays started in the schoolroom, from where their parents escorted them to the dining room to find their presents arranged on a table. In 1848 the queen records that Princess Alice was given 'a live little lamb all decked out with ribbons… We had it tamed by Toward's [the estate steward's] daughter. It is a sweet gentle little thing.' The animal painter Thomas Sidney Cooper (1803–1902) painted Milly the lamb at Barton Farm and gave the painting to the princess.

Queen Victoria's birthday table at Osborne, 24 May 1848, painted by Joseph Nash the Elder (1809–78). The two glass pedestal chandeliers given by Prince Albert are displayed in the drawing room

16 HORN ROOM

The door to the horn room on the right of the corridor has been half-glazed. It is kept closed to protect the 19th-century carpet and wallpaper. This room was the setting for some of Queen Victoria's birthday tables (see opposite page). Prince Albert bought the remarkable collection of antler furniture (attributed to F Bohler of Frankfurt) in 1845 – even the circular table is inlaid with sections of deer horn. In 1847 the royal couple stayed at Ardverikie, in Inverness, before visiting Balmoral for the first time. They brought back stags' horns which they arranged in the horn room at Osborne that September.

In 1989 Landseer's moving portrait of Queen Victoria was returned to this room, where it was first hung in 1867. Alternately titled *Osborne 1865* and *Sorrow*, it depicts the widowed queen in the broad walk at Osborne seated on her pony Flora, reading a despatch. John Brown, her Highland servant, is clad in the mourning kilt the queen devised for him. Behind, on a bench, sit Princesses Louise and Helena in lilac half-mourning dresses. The painting was exhibited at the Royal Academy in 1867, and further fuelled unfounded speculation about the queen's relationship with Brown.

In the corridor on the left are two pictures of the Georgian Osborne House, one of which was ingeniously drawn in 1844 using multi-coloured Alum Bay sand – an art form popular on the island in the 19th century.

QUEEN VICTORIA'S LIFT

This passenger lift was installed by Otis in 1893 to allow the increasingly infirm queen easier access to her first-floor apartments. She was wheeled in her 'rolling chair' into the lift which was hand-operated by an attendant in the basement. Outside the lift, in the corner, is a jib-door behind which a footman clad in livery of scarlet coat and white stockings could observe the carriage ring for signs of the queen's carriage approaching.

This corridor area was formerly a guest bedroom before it was converted into part of the corridor linking the newly built Durbar Wing of 1890–91. The dado is covered with Lincrusta, an embossed wall-covering popular at the time.

A pair of half-glazed doors pierce the original external wall of the Pavilion and lead into the Durbar Corridor, which also has a Lincrusta dado.

Left: Horn furniture similar to this was displayed in the Great Exhibition of 1851, and enjoyed increased popularity after that date
Below: The horn room was sometimes used as a visitors' sitting room

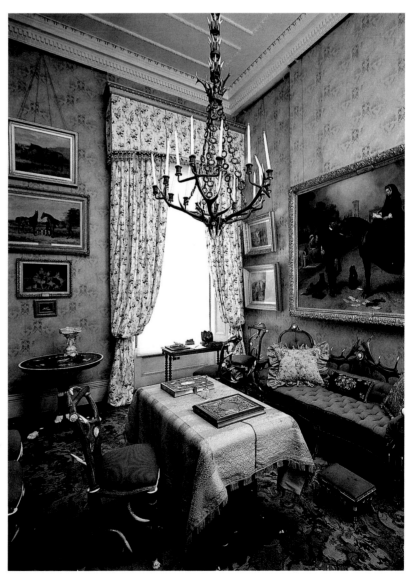

Queen Victoria and India

The queen wrote to her daughter-in-law, 'I have such a great longing to go to India… I have been thinking of it very much of late'

Queen Victoria was created empress of India by Disraeli in 1876. In 1887 her son Prince Arthur, duke of Connaught, was serving in India as commander-in-chief of the Bombay army. The queen wrote to her daughter-in-law, 'I have such a great longing to go to India…You may think me crazy for saying this – but I can assure you I have been thinking of it – very much of late.' The visit never took place, but in June 1887 the queen took on two Indian servants, the first of many, at Osborne. An extension to the male servants' barracks was constructed to house them, and in the 1890s the surveyor of works regularly recorded his men preparing curry stones for them to use.

The Indian servants wore turbans and a livery of scarlet and gold in winter and white in summer. It was embroidered with the monogram VRI (*Victoria Regina et Imperatrix* – Victoria Queen and Empress). One of these, Abdul Karim, was an ambitious 24-year-old Muslim who in 1889 was promoted to the post of *munshi*, teaching the queen Hindi. However, jealousies arose within the household, and, while Karim claimed his father was a surgeon-general in India, his status was called into question. The queen asked Frederick Ponsonby, who was appointed equerry while serving in India, to make enquiries. On his return Ponsonby told the queen, truthfully but tactlessly, that Karim's father was druggist to the gaol in Agra. The queen was deeply offended and refused to invite Ponsonby for lunch for a year.

Clockwise from top right: Portrait of Abdul Karim, Queen Victoria's Indian secretary, by Rudolf Swoboda, 1888, in the white- and gold-striped turban that the queen decreed should be worn at dinner time. The other images show fine examples of Indian craftsmanship presented to the queen by her Indian subjects: lacquerwork address case and its velvet inner cover from Hyderabad, Sind, 1887; silver elephant address casket from the Rao of Kutch, 1897; ivory workbox from the Raja of Bobbili, 1893. The gifts reveal the same intricacy of surface detail found on a larger scale in the Durbar Room

⒘ DURBAR CORRIDOR

The new wing was constructed in 1890–91 to house Prince and Princess Henry of Battenberg and their family on the first floor. Princess Henry (Beatrice) was Queen Victoria's youngest daughter. The queen was so dependent on her in later years that when Beatrice unofficially announced her engagement in 1883, the queen did not speak to her for six months. She was given permission to marry in 1885, on the understanding that she continued to live with the queen.

In the Durbar Corridor and Durbar Room, the queen could create a tangible reminder of the land that she would never visit. The paintings in the Durbar Corridor reflect the queen's interest in her Indian empire and its people. The most imposing portrait is that of the maharaja Duleep Singh, commissioned by the queen from Winterhalter in 1854. Nearby on the left-hand wall are three small paintings on porcelain of the maharaja, his wife the maharanee Bamba, and their son Victor Albert, named in honour of the royal couple.

The corridor running the length of the south side of the Durbar Wing contains a unique and extensive collection of Indian portraits painted by the Austrian portraitist Rudolf Swoboda (1859–1914). In 1886 London hosted the Colonial and Indian Exhibition, which included a living display of over 30 Indian craftsmen. Swoboda had recently been introduced to the queen and she commissioned him to paint some of those craftsmen. Enthused by his paintings, she commissioned him to go to India to sketch 'various types of different nationalities'. He travelled in India from 1886 to 1888 and produced 43 closely observed studies from life.

The portraits were hung as a group in the Durbar Corridor on its completion in 1894, together with his other portraits of some of the queen's Indian servants, including Abdul Karim – the munshi – and the designer Bhai Ram Singh. The queen considered his portraits 'beautiful things' and they form an important record of a wide cross-section of Indian society, ages and occupations.

Above: Duleep Singh, *by F X Winterhalter, 1854, commissioned in the year the 15-year-old maharaja stayed at Osborne*
Below: *A sample from one of the framed groups of Indian portraits by Rudolf Swoboda, 1886–8, in the Durbar Corridor*

🔢 DURBAR ROOM

The name is derived from an Indian word meaning both a state reception and the hall in which it is held, so the room is appropriately named both for its function and for its Indian style of architecture, which was briefly popular towards the end of the 19th century. While Prince Arthur, the duke of Connaught, was serving in India, he met Lockwood Kipling (father of Rudyard) who was director of the Mayo School of Art at Lahore in the Punjab. In 1884 the billiard room at Connaught's home, Bagshot Park, Surrey, was

Top: The peacock chimneypiece. The peacock is a common Indian motif
Right: Bhai Ram Singh from the Lahore School of Art, India, at work in the Durbar Room in 1891. He designed and carved the wooden moulds for the plasterwork. The photograph shows the exposed timber battens supporting plasterwork on the end wall

decorated in Indian style as a gift from the Indian princes. The carving was done in Lahore by Bhai Ram Singh, under the supervision of Kipling and Connaught introduced their work to the queen. In August 1890 Kipling was asked to submit an Indian design for the new room at Osborne. The queen and Princess Louise made suggestions to improve the design and in January 1891 Kipling arrived at Osborne with Ram Singh.

J R Mann's plan of the Durbar Room suggests a medieval great hall, with a screens passage and minstrels' gallery at the 'low' end, with the servery beyond. The decoration is inspired by the architectural traditions of north India – a fusion of Islamic forms with decoration from Hindu and Jain temples that is sometimes described as Indo-Saracenic, looking back to the Mogul architecture of 16th and 17th centuries. This flamboyant version includes an unusual variety of detail, effectively creating a unique room for English court protocol in the Indian style.

Ram Singh designed and carved the wooden moulds used by the plasterers, Jacksons of London. The surfaces are enriched with plaster and carton pierre – a type of papier mâché common in the late 19th century – the white walls being further enlivened by teak framing. The dado panels ornamented with vases of flowers resemble the types of *pietra dura* design (inlay using hard stones) found on the walls of Mogul monuments such as the Taj Mahal. The cornice and overmantel are ornamented with multiple niches, a form found in Indian Islamic architecture from the 12th century onwards. The wall above the screen is set with chattris, a type of domed canopy favoured in Mogul design. The decoration includes the Indian symbols of Ganesh – the elephant god of good fortune – over the door near the gallery.

Princess Louise suggested a peacock over the chimneypiece in November 1890. Jacksons had 26 craftsmen working on the chimneypiece and overmantel. More than 500 hours were spent on the peacock alone, equivalent to one man working solidly for ten weeks. The deeply coffered ceiling is derived from the ceiling ornament found in medieval temple structures such as the Jain temples at Mount Abu, Rajasthan.

Ram Singh also designed the brass door handles in the form of a bird and the brass lamp stands. In February 1893, the queen wrote,

Left: The Durbar Room, Christmas 1896, with a tree and tables of presents
Below: One of the original set of 36 dining chairs designed for the room by Bhai Ram Singh. The furniture was disposed of in 1916, but English Heritage bought nine chairs with the help of the National Art Collections Fund, the Heritage Lottery Fund, the Island Friends of Royal Osborne and the Duleep Singh Trust. Replicas have been made for visitors to use

'We dined in the Durbar Room which was lit by electric light & looked beautiful.' She was won over to electricity, and by September 1894 most of the building was lit with Edison & Swan lamps.

The room contains a new display of gifts from the sub-continent commemorating Queen Victoria's golden and diamond jubilees of 1887 and 1897. The address caskets form most of the collection – decorative boxes containing loyal greetings to the queen. They were sent from every part of the Indian empire, and provide a rare snapshot of the state of Indian craftsmanship at the end of the 19th century. One of the most beautiful is a replica of the great gun of Bijapur, a cannon cast in Agra in 1549. Some are very rare such as those decorated with sadeli work, where tiny pieces of ivory, metal and coloured woods

are inlaid in geometrical patterns. The exquisite model of a palace in Jaipur is made from plaster, painted and gilded. Even the interiors are recreated in colourful detail.

To mark the centenary of the queen's death in 2001, the collection was redisplayed in new cases. In addition, the original Indian carpet from Agra and the curtains have been copied, as has the arrangement of the lighting (with replica light bulbs) in order to recreate the appearance of the room in about 1900.

The lobby at the far end of the Durbar Room was originally a private entrance hall serving the Battenbergs' apartments. At the other end, the right-hand door beneath the minstrels' gallery leads to the former Durbar servery, which has a new visitors' exit and ramp on to the terrace.

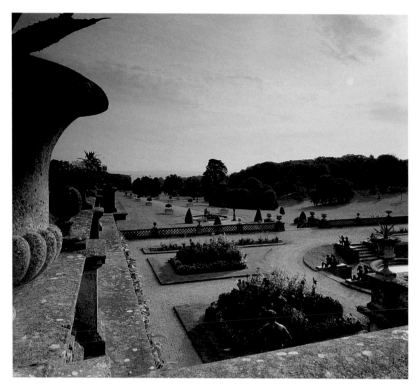

Above: View from the upper terrace of the broad walk leading down the valley to the Solent
Below: Ludwig Gruner's drawing for the sphinx vase on the Pavilion terrace, 1849. Gruner also designed other ornaments for the terraces and acted as the prince's agent in buying some of the cement statuary

TERRACES

Gruner helped to design and lay out the Italianate terraces at the head of the valley with Prince Albert and Cubitt. Massive earth-moving was needed and the valley was remodelled to create the sweeping fall to the coast. Some of the terrace retaining walls are up to 7.6m (25ft) deep.

Pavilion Terrace

Gruner took items from Austin & Seeley's 1844 catalogue and arranged them to create a huge vase comprising four sphinxes with added wings supporting a fluted bowl. He also bought the surrounding statues of the Four Seasons supplied by Miroy Frères of Paris, and copies of Florentine and Roman originals from the catalogue of Geiss of Berlin, to enhance Osborne's Italianate qualities. In the salt-laden air the applied bronze corroded

to reveal the zinc beneath, which in turn became pitted by the salts. The statues have now been recoated with a reversible acrylic compound to imitate the original patinated bronze.

The projecting square alcove to the left of the clock tower was used by Queen Victoria for breakfast, and for reading and writing.

The parterres on the terrace were initially framed by walkways of coloured imitation lava from Orsi & Armani of London. There was a rich variety of bedding plants: the queen writes in her journal of geraniums, heliotropes and the summer evening air scented with orange blossom, roses and jasmine. Excavations in 1994 uncovered the chalk footings to the elaborate beds which follow those on a mid-19th-century plan in the National Archives, and these have now been re-created. Historic bedding has been reinstated, using, where possible, plants introduced to Britain before the queen's death.

Lower Terrace

The lower terrace contains a triple-arched alcove flanked by steps. The shell alcove nearby has a canal-coal bench with dolphin supports and is decorated with shells from the beach. Queen Victoria records a delightful observation in August 1852 of workmen fixing shells to the roof while a 'charming magpie' was taking all the shells. In the middle of the lower terrace is the Andromeda fountain by John Bell, surrounded by eight marine monsters by William Theed, cast in 1858–60. Other statues are copies of classical originals, including the hunter Meleager with his spear and hound.

Austin & Seeley's cement copies of the Medici lions in Florence, supplied in 1851, flank the lowest flight of steps beyond the fountain. The lions face the lowest fountain of a bronze boy with a swan, from Geiss of Berlin. It sits at the head of the broad walk which has planters, reinstated in 2005, of clipped Portuguese laurel (*Prunus lusitanica*), as shown in Landseer's painting *Sorrow* (see page 46).

Upper Terrace

The horseshoe steps at the far end of the upper terrace lead down to a further lower terrace opposite the former orangery and Victoria Hall (both now part of the terrace restaurant). The orangery doors are white, unlike the rest of the external doors and windows of the main house which are red in imitation of mahogany. The cast heads in the keystones have all been adapted by Cubitt so that each is different; one on the right bears a strong resemblance to Prince Albert.

The adjoining Victoria hall was originally a blind wall to screen the stable block and other service buildings. In the 1880s, the arches were opened and a private chapel built behind so that the increasingly infirm queen could avoid services at Whippingham. It is now the terrace restaurant, where the stained glass and inscription above the chimneypiece indicate its original function.

Against the outside wall is the royal myrtle (*Myrtus communis*) grown from a sprig from the nosegay presented by the dowager duchess of Saxe Gotha and Attenburg (Prince Albert's grandmother) to Queen Victoria on leaving Gotha, 3 September 1845. It has since been used in royal wedding bouquets as a symbol of the innocence of the bride, a German tradition.

Other significant plants here include the chusan palm (*Trachycarpus fortunei*), planted by the queen on her birthday in 1851, one of the first to be planted out-of-doors in this country. It was felled due to old age and Queen Elizabeth II planted a replacement on the 20 May 2004. The walls of the lower terrace are also clothed with *Magnolia grandiflora* planted by Prince Albert.

On the low wall nearby are two artificial stone greyhounds flanking the path. The sloping walk beyond this wall leads up to the Swiss Cottage drive. It contains a granite memorial bench on the yew walk, south of the orangery, where John Brown apparently used to read his letters from home. It is carved with a relief of Brown and an inscription suggested by Tennyson: 'A truer, nobler trustier heart, more loving and more loyal, never beat within a human breast.' The queen chose the quotation from a play by Byron, *The Two Foscari*, where – curiously – it is said by a wife in defence of her maligned husband.

Above: One of the pair of greyhounds with lead claws, supplied by Austin & Seeley in 1856
Below: The Andromeda fountain and clocktower seen from the Pavilion terrace. Queen Victoria's mother occupied a ground-floor suite to the right of the clocktower

John Brown

'I feel I have
here always in the
House a good,
devoted Soul ...
whose only
object & interest
is my service ...'

John Brown (1826–83) was born in Crathienaird, Aberdeenshire, son of a tenant farmer. He came into the queen's service in 1848 as a gillie at Balmoral. By 1858 he had become her regular outside attendant, leading her pony on their Highland expeditions, helping cook potatoes on the moors, and lacing her tea with whisky.

The queen was so overwhelmed by the death of the prince consort that she did not attend a public function until 1864. There was considerable concern for her health, so in 1864 it was suggested that Brown might be brought to Osborne to encourage her to ride her pony. He arrived in December, and the queen soon made the arrangement permanent, giving Brown the title 'the queen's Highland servant'. She wrote, 'I feel I have here always in the House a good, devoted Soul… whose only object & interest is my service, & God knows how much I want to be taken care of.'

But Brown's forthright manner made him enemies and he could be blunt to the point of rudeness: the lord chamberlain dismissed him as a 'coarse animal'. Brown would address the queen as 'wumman', but she overlooked his faults, including his increasing over-dependence on whisky which, to use her euphemism, made him 'bashful'. Given the nature of the queen's relative seclusion in the 1870s it is easy to see how unfounded rumours spread of Brown's relationship to the queen, the mildest of which was their supposed marriage.

The queen was inconsolable after Brown's death in March 1883: 'It is the loss not only of a servant but of a real friend.' Sir Henry Ponsonby, her private secretary, wrote a balanced view: 'He was the only person who could fight and make the Queen do what she did not wish. He did not always succeed, nor was his advice always the best. But I believe he was honest, and with all his want of education, his roughness, his prejudices, and other faults, he was undoubtedly a most excellent servant to her.'

John Brown in his grey Osborne kilt, devised by the queen as a form of half-mourning in 1861. Queen Victoria commissioned the watercolour by Kenneth MacLeay (1802–78) as part of a series called Highlanders of Scotland, published in two volumes in 1870. The queen gave a set to John Brown that Christmas

WALLED GARDEN AND PLEASURE GROUNDS

The walled kitchen garden and adjoining pleasure grounds in front of the house remain as elements from the late 18th-century landscape. In 1843 the garden was described as 'fully cropped and stocked with choice standard and other trees', but towards the end of Queen Victoria's reign the emphasis was on growing flowers for the house. The original cross-path layout has been restored and a new garden added in 2000, to the design of Rupert Goldby. It incorporates trained Victorian fruit trees such as Lane's Prince Albert apples, Victoria plums and Brunswick figs, while further period fruit and roses overhang the new iron arches framing the paths. A cold-frame in the north-east corner is full in winter and spring with Queen Victoria's favourite Parma violets.

The two Gothic lean-to glasshouses were erected in 1854 by Thomas Clark & Co of Birmingham. They copy the formerly extensive range of glasshouses erected for Prince Albert at Frogmore, Windsor, in the 1840s.

Near the walled garden is a small timber octagonal summerhouse built by Cubitt in 1848. The children occasionally had their supper there. Cubitt heightened the front wall in 1848. He disguised the brick buttresses to look like stone pilasters and in the centre he placed the Portland stone entrance porch salvaged from the demolished house.

Albert improved the pleasure grounds, where the family would stroll, by planting magnolias, rhododendrons and azaleas around the summerhouse. The walk along Swiss Cottage Drive follows the contours of the valley and provides an excellent view of Osborne and its terraces, as well as passing close to the ice house. The formal landscape around the house is in marked contrast to the parkland through which the visitor now passes.

Trees

By 1861, the estate had 400 acres of woodland, principally around the park. The woodland was commercially managed, providing products such as hurdles and rods for fencing. Walks and rides were cut and ornamented for use by the royal family. Restoration is now taking place of views and vistas.

Throughout the park and pleasure grounds, an important visit, anniversary, or birth or death might be commemorated by planting a memorial tree, of which at least 270 existed across the estate. Many were new introductions to Britain.

Prince Albert's planting scheme was partially dictated by his respect for the well-established late 18th-century landscape of old Osborne house. Other influences included his liking for the poplars at the Rosenau and for the Italian fashion of lining drives and walks with evergreens such as myrtle and laurel. Barton Drive is planted with holm oak (*Quercus ilex*), which gives a Mediterranean feel to the curved avenue. The Sovereign's Drive is a double avenue of cedar of Lebanon and *Quercus*

'*Lucombeana*' (outer) and holm oak (inner).

Albert was intensely practical, and the flag tower of the Pavilion provided a vantage point from which he could direct gardeners in the positioning of flags to represent trees in the parkland. He strengthened the shelter-belt of broad-leafed woodland in the outer park along the coast where native trees – oak, elm and beech – predominated. He left a clear view of the Solent either side of the valley to frame the house when seen from the sea, which was centred on the main wing, the site of old Osborne house.

Ice House

Ice was used to prepare food and to cool the dining room. The ice house was built by Cubitt in 1846 into the side of the hill, with a cavity wall for insulation. The floor is lined with bricks drilled with holes to drain melting ice. On 14 December 1846 the queen wrote, 'Went to see the ice house filled which is quite a curious performance. Hardest frost we have yet had. The men were breaking it above and throwing it down through an opening – we watched from below, ice falling like rain.' In the harsh winter of 1859, 60 cartloads of ice were packed into the ice house over two days. A classical entrance was added in 1853.

Facing page: The porch of the demolished old Osborne house became the entrance to the walled garden

Above: *The walled garden in summer*

Below: *The classical entrance to the ice house. The supply of ice on the estate was unreliable and the queen preferred lake ice imported from the USA*

SWISS COTTAGE GARDEN

The grounds around the Swiss Cottage were conceived as part of Prince Albert's educational programme for his children. Many aspects of the disciplined regime of his own childhood were recreated here, including a children's garden, a Swiss cottage, a museum and model fort.

The area was given to the royal children in 1850. Each child had a plot where he or she could grow soft fruits and vegetables to sell at commercial rates to Prince Albert as a practical exercise in market gardening. The gardens were left as the children had them until 1905, when they were given over to flowers.

A thatched summerhouse opposite the Swiss cottage contains replicas of the children's scaled-down garden tools and barrows, each painted with its owner's initials. It also contains a swing which hung from a nearby tree. The building was rethatched with long straw in 2003, in imitation of the 19th-century pattern, with crossed hazel 'liggers'.

Fruit and vegetables are now grown again in the children's gardens, which are primarily maintained organically. All the varieties would have been available in the 19th century, and the vegetables are often allowed to run to seed so that old varieties which are no longer available commercially can be propagated.

Wildflower Garden and Gazelle House

Beyond the Swiss Cottage is a large paddock, which has been managed as a wildflower area for the past 100 years. The historic orchard has also been reinstated, displaying a full range of old varieties of culinary apples and pears, cherries, plums and gages, quince, medlar, mulberry and nuts. The fountain on a Portland stone base within the wildflower garden was added for the benefit of visitors by the Office of Works in 1907. The lead statue and basin were cast from models made by the designer Felix Joubert, of the fashionable Chelsea cabinet-makers and decorators.

Nearby is the timber gazelle house first constructed in the 1860s and replaced in 1872. The animals were bred there and formed part of a small menagerie. In later years, a large colony of Angora rabbits in numerous hutches were housed in the paddock. Their wool was used by Princess Beatrice who spun and wove it into items to be sent to local bazaars.

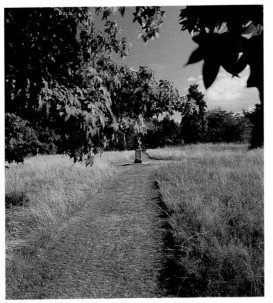

Facing page: The frieze of the Swiss Cottage is carved with improving quotations in German including, 'You will carry your load more easily if you add patience to the burden'

Top: The Swiss Cottage with rocks on the roof. These imitate a real Alpine building, where they prevent the wind from lifting the roof. They were removed in 1932 and some can be seen built into the bank beside the visitor WCs.

Middle: The royal children's original garden tools and barrows in the summerhouse. Modern copies are now displayed

Bottom: The wildflower garden has been managed in this way for 100 years

The Swiss Cottage in 1855 by W L Leitch. The inspiration for a Swiss cottage may have come from Queen Victoria's half-sister, Princess Feodore of Hoehenlohe Langenberg, who wrote to the queen in 1851 that she had constructed a little Swiss cottage for her children in the garden of the Villa Friesenberg at Baden-Baden. An Alpine chalet dating from the 1830s with German quotations is also a feature of Shrubland, Suffolk, which Prince Albert visited in 1851

SWISS COTTAGE

In 1853 the royal children laid the foundation stone of a timber Swiss cottage to the east of Osborne house. It sits on a rubble plinth and originally had a timber roof weighted down with rocks in the Alpine manner. The furnished cottage was given to the princes and princesses on Queen Victoria's birthday in 1854.

The first-floor balcony and other details imitate a traditional Swiss farmhouse. It has a frieze carved in German with proverbs and quotations from the Psalms, doubtless intended by Prince Albert as precepts to guide his children through life. The external logs were coated with burnt umber which is deep brown in colour. They were covered with black tar in the 20th century and have now been repainted brown.

In 1867 it was claimed that the Swiss Cottage was built 'in exact imitation of a Swiss chalet, and the furniture, ornaments, and decoration for it, were expressly imported from Switzerland'. However, the evidence suggests otherwise. It was designed in imperial measurements, with principal dimensions of 25 x 50ft (6.6 x 15.2m). Metal fixings were applied instead of using the logs in a

structural way. Analysis in 1990 suggested that the logs are *Pinus strobus*, a long-leafed pine found in North America. The Swiss Cottage may, therefore, have been prefabricated in England and re-erected at Osborne by local carpenters under the supervision of the surveyor of works John Blandford (d.1857). But the cast-iron casement windows may well have been imported as the circular glazing pattern is very rare in England. A plan and elevation of the cottage dated 1856 is signed 'G.S.', who has so far avoided identification.

Prince Albert intended the Swiss Cottage to be somewhere his children could learn the rudiments of housekeeping and cookery and entertain their parents. As boys, he and his brother Ernest had created a natural-history museum in Coburg. Albert set aside a room at the Swiss Cottage where his children could build a similar collection. Objects came from all over the world, and the collection grew so that a separate museum was built nearby in 1862.

Louise Warne, housekeeper at the cottage, lived with her husband on the ground floor. Among her duties was to look after a chihuahua presented in 1856, which the queen described as 'a curious little dog brought from Mexico – something like a diminutive Italian greyhound'.

The first room on the ground floor is the pantry. It has a fireplace with a cast-iron grate and small boiler, with a built-in sink under the window. A dresser holds the dinner service used during Queen Victoria's lifetime. In the adjoining kitchen is a small-scale mid-19th-century Belgian range and charcoal burners.

The first floor is reached via external stairs and a balcony. The children frequently took tea in the dining room and Queen Victoria visited, using the writing desk on the left-hand wall on which sit quills, headed writing paper, a blotting book and silver seal stamped 'Swiss Cottage'. On the rear wall is an ornately carved secretaire, reputedly of Swiss manufacture, as is the model of a Swiss clockmaker on the mantelpiece. Most of the furniture on this floor is English, including the remarkable American birch furniture with bobbin-turned legs. It was made for the Swiss Cottage by the local Newport firm of Francis Pittis in 1854, and includes the dining table (with five extra leaves in a stand), chairs, and fire screen. An octagonal work table has a silver label stating that it was designed by the king of the Sandwich Islands and given to Queen Victoria by his widow Queen Emma.

The lobby has two cloak stands, also by Pittis, as were the wardrobe, washstand, mirror, and a cane-seated couch in the dressing room on the left.

The sitting room was the first location of the museum. It contains a remarkable model shop, named 'Spratt, Grocer to her Majesty'.

Above: The kitchen is lined with blue and white tiles and has a small Belgian range
Left: The dining room. Under a glass dome on the table is a carved basket of flowers presented to the queen by Iroquois Indians from North America

Top: The Bulgarian orphans' clothes are in the case on the right. The boys were rescued during the Crimean war from Constanta (now Romania) bordering the Black Sea
Centre: *The museum. The cases are original but the arrangement is from 1916*
Bottom: *Victoria Fort and the brick-built Albert Barracks, probably built at the suggestion of Prince Albert, who used to play in mock forts with his brother*

MUSEUM

The Swiss museum was built in 1862 to house the collections which had outgrown the Swiss Cottage. It is also timber, but with a slate roof, and lacks the elaborate detailing of the Swiss Cottage. The cases are original, but Sir Guy Laking (keeper of the king's armoury and curator of the Museum of London) re-arranged the contents in 1916, and his distinctive gold labels remain.

Geological specimens (cases 21–30, 34–39), shells (42) – many from Osborne beach – and stuffed animal and birds (31–33, 40–41) are assembled here, along with mementos of foreign tours including antiquities (3–8) and rare items from the North American Micmac Indians, acquired by the prince of Wales during his tour of 1860 (9).

Case 12 contains the clothes of two Bulgarian orphans, Johens and Georgy, who, aged four years and 15 months respectively, were rescued by the British Navy having been wounded by the Turks in the Crimean war in 1854. Queen Victoria took pity on the boys, who were brought up by Ann Jackman, the wife of a carter on the Osborne estate, in one of the Barton cottages.

VICTORIA FORT AND ALBERT BARRACKS

Near the museum is a miniature earth fort with redoubts that was built against the political backdrop of the Crimean war. Russia invaded Turkey in 1853, and France and Britain, fearful of Russian expansion, declared war on Russia in March 1854. But it was not until September 1855 that the Russians evacuated Sebastopol, and the war did not end until 30 March 1856, with the signing of the treaty of Paris. The appalling conditions of the British soldiers as reported in *The Times* caused a public outcry, which eventually led to a number of nurses, headed by Florence Nightingale, being sent to the hospital at Scutari.

Victoria Fort was completed in 1856, within two months of the signing of the treaty. The Prince of Wales (Bertie) and Prince Alfred (Affie) helped build it as a birthday surprise for Queen Victoria under the direction of Prince Alfred's governor, Lieutenant Cowell of the Royal Engineers. In 1860 the 10-year-old Prince Arthur – later to become Field Marshal the duke of Connaught – helped add the brick-built Albert Barracks inside the fort. A drawbridge was added in 1861.

QUEEN VICTORIA'S BATHING MACHINE

The prince was a believer in the benefits of sea bathing, and the proximity of the beach was significant in his choice of Osborne. The bathing machine ran on stone rails into the sea. Queen Victoria recorded her first experience of sea bathing on 30 July 1847: 'Drove down to the beach with my maids and went into the bathing machine, where I undressed and bathed in the sea (for the first time in my life), a very nice bathing woman attending me. I thought it delightful till I put my head under the water, when I thought I should be stifled.' After her death, the bathing machine was used as a chicken shed. It was moved in 1927, but restored only in the 1950s.

The children learnt to swim in a floating bath apparently devised by Prince Albert, and built by John and Robert White of Cowes in 1854. A wood grating suspended between two pontoons could be raised or lowered according to the height of the swimmer. Because of the 4m tidal range, it was moored 60m off Osborne Bay, where it was accessed via a small boat manned by a pair of sailors from the royal yacht. Prince Albert frequently took the older princes for a daily swim, while some of the princesses were taught by Eugene Loby, a young woman from Boulogne. The floating bath was finally broken up by a storm in 1900. The model for it survives.

ALBERTA DECKHOUSE

The deckhouse comes from the royal steam yacht *Alberta* which replaced the *Fairy* as a tender to the royal yacht *Victoria & Albert*. The *Alberta* was constructed by the Admiralty at Pembroke dockyard, and launched in 1864. The paddle steamer had a complement of 25 men, was 106ft (32.3m) long and had a beam of 22ft (6.7m), and weighed 391 tons (397 metric tons); she was capable of reaching a speed of 14 knots.

The *Alberta* was regularly used by Queen Victoria on her journeys between Gosport and the Isle of Wight. The *Alberta* also carried her body back to the mainland for its journey to the royal mausoleum in January 1901.

The deckhouse spent many years as a garden shed in Portsmouth until rescued by the Navy and given to Osborne in the 1970s.

Left: The queen's bathing machine (left), with some of the original stone rails brought from the beach, and the Alberta deckhouse

History

The house and estate created by
Queen Victoria and Prince Albert
at Osborne are unrivalled in terms
of the intimate insight they can
give into the private life of the
country's longest-reigning monarch.
The story of a marriage, a family
and an empire is told in the richly
decorated rooms and the treasures
they contain. The tranquil gardens
and wider landscape were vitally
important for a couple seeking an
escape from court life.

READING THE HISTORY

*This section describes how Queen Victoria and
Prince Albert developed the house and estate.
It gives an account of informal royal family life at
Osborne and the impact of the death of Prince Albert
in 1861. The History covers the years after the
queen's death: occupation of Osborne by a
Royal Naval College and a convalescent home, and
recent restoration by English Heritage.*

OSBORNE HOUSE

When Queen Victoria married Prince Albert of Saxe-Coburg in 1840, she had three palaces to live in: Windsor Castle, Buckingham Palace and the Royal Pavilion at Brighton. These soon proved unsuitable to the parents of a growing family, so in October 1843 the couple sought a country house. They wanted, to use the queen's words, 'a place of one's own, quiet and retired'.

The queen knew and liked the Isle of Wight, and the expanding railway network would enable the couple to journey to the island from Buckingham Palace or Windsor in under four hours. The prime minister, Sir Robert Peel, sympathetically promoted her enquiries, which led her to the Osborne estate. The couple visited Osborne in 1844. The queen wrote: 'It is impossible to imagine a prettier spot – we have a charming beach quite to ourselves – we can walk anywhere without being followed or mobbed.'

The house was of brick and stone, of three storeys with a canted bay overlooking the Solent. It had been remodelled from an earlier house by 'Mr Sanderson' (probably the London architect John Sanderson) who in August 1774 supplied a plan for alterations to the then owner Robert Pope Blachford (1742–90). Blachford's brick-walled kitchen garden to the west and a brick stable block to the south survive, but all that remains of the 1770s house is the Portland stone porch, re-sited in about 1850 as a grand entrance to the 1770s kitchen garden.

In 1844 the queen wrote, 'I am delighted with the house, all over which we went. The rooms are small but very nice. With some few alterations and additions for the children it might be made an excellent house.' The queen sought *Gemütlichkeit* ('snugness' or 'cosiness'), but the lack of space she identified was a major problem and more extensive building works would be required.

Prince Albert, who once complained that he was 'the husband not master of the house', recognised that Osborne would enable him to indulge creatively some of his many passions: estate management, agricultural improvement, building, landscape design, gardening and education. It is clear from Queen Victoria's journal that Albert was heavily involved with all aspects creating the new house and estate – in 1848 she referred to him as 'Albert the Creator'.

Above: Old Osborne house, by C R Stanley, 1844
Below: Engraving in the audience room of Thomas Cubitt, from a painting by H W Pickersgill (1782–1875)

Facing page: Prince Albert in the uniform of a colonel of the Rifle Brigade, by F X Winterhalter, 1859

The queen bought the estate in May 1845 using her privy purse for the bargain price of a little under £28,000. Thomas Cubitt, the London builder and developer of entire suburbs in Pimlico, Bloomsbury and Belgravia, was engaged – 'such an honest, kind, good man', noted the queen.

Cubitt provided drawings and supervised the work. Much of the joinery and cast iron was manufactured in his London workshops. Bricks were made on the estate and the whole building was rendered with local Medina cement, the top coat coloured to imitate warm Bath stone. The recent exterior restoration by English Heritage replicates the original colour.

The Pavilion was the first part to be built, and the family moved in in September 1846. Cubitt's workmen did not undertake any 'gilding or fancy painting' and he often left the rooms with green 'builder's finish' on the walls – a distemper which could be washed off later. Much of the Italian *cinquecento*-style internal decoration was designed under the guidance of Professor Ludwig Gruner of Dresden (1801–82), who had been appointed the queen's 'adviser in art' in 1845. He was an authority on Raphael and Italian frescos. The

Left: A gardener in the pleasure grounds, c.1873, by Jabez Hughes (1819–84). He is standing in front of a Magnolia grandiflora *planted by Prince Albert on 10 March 1846*
Below: Watercolour by Queen Victoria of the Pavilion from the valley footpath, made c.1848 under the instruction of W L Leitch

Facing page, top: Watercolour by W L Leitch showing Osborne in 1850 before the Durbar Wing was built
Facing page, bottom: Osborne House under construction, August 1847, by W L Leitch. The main wing is not yet built and the terraces are being levelled

couple were pleased with the Italian effect. During the hot summer of 1852, the queen described the 'calm deep blue sea, the balmy air, all quite Italian'. The design had considerable influence in the United Kingdom and elsewhere; for example, the Italianate design of Government House, Melbourne, Australia, built in the 1870s, shares many features with Osborne, including a prominent flag tower.

THE ESTATE

To make the estate viable, further purchases were made, including the adjacent 500-acre Barton Manor from Winchester College, to serve as the home farm. Barton Manor (now in private ownership) dated from the early 17th century, although built on the site of an Augustinian oratory founded in 1275. By 1864 the total landholding rose to more than 2,000 acres.

Prince Albert was concerned with every aspect of the development of the estate. In his own words, in February 1847, he was 'partly forrester, partly builder, partly farmer and partly gardener'. He wrote of his enthusiasm in the winter of 1859 to Vicky, now married to

Prince Frederick William of Prussia: 'We had a fall of nine inches of snow, which looked wonderfully beautiful. I have all but broken my arms against the trees and shrubs, in clearing them, with poles, of the snow, which would otherwise have wholly crushed the fine evergreens and threatens to make havoc with the cypresses especially.'

Albert laid out the drives and paths, achieving privacy by forming bends in the principal drives to hide the house. A circular carriage ride ran near the perimeter of the estate around which the queen and prince often rode in a post-chaise. Charabancs were used when the whole family or visitors were given a tour of the park.

Barton Manor, the biggest farm, became a model of the latest agricultural methods. Cubitt thoroughly 'restored' the manor house and reorganised its outbuildings as a model farm to supply Osborne with daily produce. Farm machinery was harnessed to a portable steam engine. On the estate, awkward fields were squared off and new

roads laid out. To improve the soil the prince and Andrew Toward, estate bailiff or steward, carried out under-draining using pipe tiles which, in the 1840s, were increasingly mass-produced. By 1864 over 360 miles of drains had been constructed at an average depth of 1.2m (4ft).

Prince Albert's interests in technology, economy, and environmentally friendly estate management came together with his experiments in designing and constructing a brick-lined gravity tank to convert sewage into farm manure by filtering it through clay, sand and charcoal. From 1850 he worked with the chemist Dr Lyon Playfair (1818–98), and that year he read a paper on the subject to the Royal Agricultural Society. At Osborne the 9m-long (30ft) tank was sited on the north side of the valley as it took a steep fall of land for it to work. Prince Albert's invention was not as universally applicable as he would have wished, but the tank at Osborne remained in operation throughout the 19th century.

Right: A plan of the Osborne estate. The English Heritage boundary is in red, representing only a fraction of the 2,000 acres (810ha) bought by Queen Victoria

Facing page: An aerial view of the house and terrace gardens from the north-east

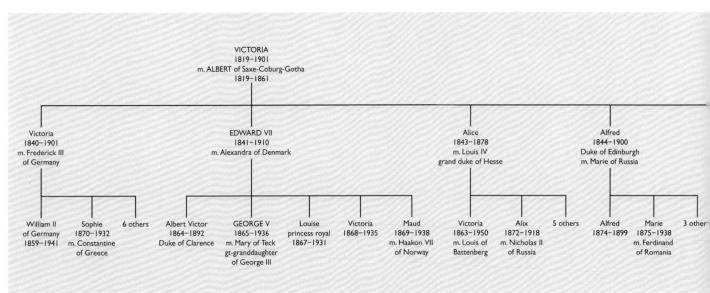

VICTORIA
1819–1901
m. ALBERT of Saxe-Coburg-Gotha
1819–1861

| Victoria
1840–1901
m. Frederick III
of Germany | | | EDWARD VII
1841–1910
m. Alexandra of Denmark | | | | | Alice
1843–1878
m. Louis IV
grand duke of Hesse | | | Alfred
1844–1900
Duke of Edinburgh
m. Marie of Russia | | |

| William II
of Germany
1859–1941 | Sophie
1870–1932
m. Constantine
of Greece | 6 others | Albert Victor
1864–1892
Duke of Clarence | GEORGE V
1865–1936
m. Mary of Teck
gt-granddaughter
of George III | Louise
princess royal
1867–1931 | Victoria
1868–1935 | Maud
1869–1938
m. Haakon VII
of Norway | Victoria
1863–1950
m. Louis of
Battenberg | Alix
1872–1918
m. Nicholas II
of Russia | 5 others | Alfred
1874–1899 | Marie
1875–1938
m. Ferdinand
of Romania | 3 other |

THE FAMILY

The royal family took delight in returning to their seaside home and each year spent as much time as possible here and at Balmoral. Queen Victoria spent a record total of 123 days at Osborne in 1848, when building and planting activity was at its height. The family, accompanied by the Court, established a regular pattern of visits by 1850, which generally included four main periods at Osborne: in March, May, part of July and August, and late November and December, leaving for Windsor just before Christmas.

Hot summer days and Queen Victoria's liking for fresh air encouraged a routine which included breakfasting outside as often as possible. Both the queen and prince enjoyed walking and riding around the park, and it was rare for them to stay indoors all day. The queen's references in her journal to reading and writing under the trees or in a small tent, taking tea in the summerhouse or with the children at the Swiss Cottage, and Albert planting or visiting Barton Farm, conceal the daily stream of dispatch-boxes and papers.

During the day, the queen would often hear the children recite French or help them with other lessons, and most evenings they would visit her in the sitting room in rotation, starting with the youngest. Prince Albert delighted in being with his children and the queen's journal frequently refers to his activities with them: giving them a magic lantern show, showing them how to catch

butterflies in a net, flying kites, or demonstrating somersaults in the hay. Winter attractions included ice-skating on the pond near Barton Farm or helping the children make snowmen. The children in turn often acted tableaux or charades before their parents, involving elaborate dressing up.

The couple hosted many royal visits there. Most were relations in some form, so they were largely family affairs. Of the remainder, the most successful visit was that of the emperor and empress of France, Napoleon III and Eugénie, in August 1857, which was informal to a degree that would have been impossible in London or Windsor, but in diplomatic terms it helped to cement the alliance between the two countries following the Crimean war. Personally, the queen was particularly captivated by the empress, and they remained close friends thereafter.

Left: The children enacting a tableau of the four seasons as a surprise for the queen and prince on their 10th wedding anniversary at Windsor Castle, 10 February 1854, by Roger Fenton (1819–69). Left to right: Alice as Spring, the Princess Royal and Arthur as Summer, Helena as a Spirit Empress, Alfred as Autumn, Louise and the prince of Wales as Winter

Below: The family near the orangery on 26 May 1857 photographed by Leonida Caldesi (1822–91). Left to right: Alfred, 12; Prince Albert, 37; Helena, 11; Arthur, 7; Alice, 14; Beatrice, six weeks; Queen Victoria, 38, princess royal, 16; Louise, 9; Leopold, 4; prince of Wales, 15

Facing page: Queen Victoria and her family by F X Winterhalter, 1847. In 1901 the original was sent to Buckingham Palace and a copy inserted in the frame in the dining room

FAMILY TREE SHOWING THE CHILDREN AND GRANDCHILDREN OF QUEEN VICTORIA AND PRINCE ALBERT

Helena 1846–1923 m. Christian of Schleswig-Holstein	Louise 1846–1939 m. John duke of Argyll	Arthur 1850–1942 Duke of Connaught m. Louise Margaret of Prussia	Leopold 1853–1884 Duke of Albany m. Helena of Waldeck	Beatrice 1857–1944 m. Henry of Battenberg
5 children		Margaret 1882–1920 m. Gustav VI of Sweden · 2 others	Alice 1883–1981 Countess of Athlone · Charles	Victoria Eugenie 'Ena' 1887–1969 m. Alfonso XIII of Spain · 3 others

Above: Osborne 1865
or Sorrow, *by Sir Edwin
Landseer, which hangs in the
horn room. All the figures
sat for Landseer in 1865,
but he also used photographs
taken at Osborne to aid his
composition. The painting was
not begun until 1867*

The Death of Albert

The prince's constitution was frail and he
constantly drove himself too hard. Writing to his
eldest daughter, the empress of Prussia, in 1859,
he complained wearily of the 'treadmill of
never-ending business. The donkey in Carisbrooke,
which you remember, is my true counterpart.
He, too, would rather munch thistles in the Castle
Moat, than turn round in the wheel at the Castle
Well; and small are the thanks he gets for his
labours.' 1861 was a devastating year for Queen
Victoria. Her mother died in March, and the
year ended with the increasing illness and finally
the death of the prince consort from typhoid at
Windsor on 14 December.

The widowed queen was overwhelmed with
grief and immediately retreated to Osborne,
supported by all her daughters (apart from Vicky
who was confined in Berlin). Her uncle Leopold,
king of the Belgians, met her there, as did Albert's
brother, Duke Ernest from Coburg. As the
despatch boxes mounted, Arthur Helps, the privy
council secretary, summoned a privy council
meeting on 6 January 1862. The queen did not

see her ministers, who 'were in dear Albert's
room, & I in mine with the door open.'

The queen remained at Osborne until early
March 1862. She never ceased to mourn. She
generally wore black, with a white widow's cap,
and her writing paper and envelopes were thickly
bordered with black. The prince's influence
governed much of her later life. As she wrote in
December 1861 '*His* wishes – *his* plans – about
everything, *his* views about *every* thing are to be
my *law*! And no human power will make me
swerve from what he decided and wished.'
Her annual routine changed, however, as the
queen appears to have avoided the associations
of earlier anniversaries. She generally returned
to Osborne in mid-December after visiting the
prince consort's mausoleum at Frogmore. Her stay
at Osborne now included Christmas, but never her
birthday on 24 May, which was almost invariably
spent at Balmoral, as was Albert's birthday in
August. Conversely, her wedding anniversary,
formerly celebrated at Buckingham Palace or
Windsor was subsequently observed at Osborne
almost every year for the rest of her life.

THE LATER YEARS

The daily running of the queen's affairs required a considerable amount of assistance. Her principal dresser, Miss Marianne Skerrett, who entered service in 1837, was also her confidante. After the death of Albert, Princess Alice and, later, Princess Beatrice partially fulfilled that role. Beatrice, Queen Victoria's youngest daughter, became her constant companion, remaining with her family in the Durbar Wing after the early death of her husband, Prince Henry of Battenberg, in 1896.

Sir Henry Ponsonby (1825–95) was the most prominent of the queen's private secretaries, Albert having fulfilled this role until his death. Ponsonby was appointed equerry to Prince Albert in 1856, and to the queen in 1861. In 1870 he became her private secretary, and from 1878 keeper of the privy purse as well. His diplomacy made him an indispensable link between the queen and her ministers, and even her children. He died on the estate in 1895 and is buried in St Mildred's, Whippingham.

Arthur Ponsonby, one of his sons and his biographer, commented, 'From my birth until his death my father seemed always to be writing and never have any holidays.' But Ponsonby's diaries do not harp on the constant demands made on him; instead, they are scattered with references to playing croquet in the summer, and skating and ice hockey in the winter with the royal princesses. An eye had to be kept out for the queen who apparently disapproved of ice hockey. If her

outrider in livery and top hat was spotted, the sticks would hurriedly be thrown in to the bank and the whole company turned innocently to figure-skating.

The queen was renowned for her imperviousness to the cold. Lord Clarendon (1800–70), several times foreign secretary, visited Osborne in 1860 and complained of the queen playing the 'royal game of summer worse than ever – all the windows were open and all the noses were blue at and after dinner last night, and today, tho' people are shivering, the Queen I understand doubts whether it is not too hot to drive to Freshwater'. Cubitt's heating system provided background warmth, but it also relied on

Above: Queen Victoria at Frogmore working outside with one of her Indian servants in attendance. She used a similar tent at Osborne

Below: The queen and some of her family at Osborne, 1898. Left to right: Prince Leopold of Battenberg, Princess Aribert of Anhalt, duchess of York with Prince Edward and Princess Mary (on knee), Princess Margaret of Connaught, Prince Alexander of Battenberg (on ground), duke of York with Prince Albert, Queen Victoria, Prince Arthur of Connaught, duchess of Connaught, Princess Patricia of Connaught (on ground), Princess Henry of Battenberg, Princess Ena of Battenberg, Princess Helena Victoria of Schleswig-Holstein, Prince Maurice of Battenberg

Right: Watercolour of Queen
Victoria on her deathbed,
24 January 1901, by Hubert
von Herkomer (1849–1914).
The artist was commissioned
by a newspaper and given
permission by the king to
make the drawing. The queen,
draped with white lace, wore
her wedding veil and held
the tortoiseshell cross which
formerly hung above her bed.
The bed was strewn with
lilies, which gave a strong
scent to the room

fires in the rooms. The queen preferred to burn
beech logs and had a dislike of coal. (Even Prince
Albert, writing to his eldest daughter one morning
in September 1858, confessed, 'Osborne is green
and beautiful, but the weather cold and stormy.
Mama will be much hurt when she gets up and
finds I have had a fire lit.') Marie Mallett, a
lady-in-waiting, wrote in January 1891: 'The house
is fairly warm, but the Drawing Room so
"Siberian" and I came to bed chilled to the bone.'

Some evenings were enlivened by lectures,
recitals or theatricals, which the queen termed
'treats'. In 1866 the pianist Hallé stayed to play for
the queen. Others who performed at Osborne
included Signor Tosti, Dame Clara Butt and Dame
Nellie Melba, and theatrical performances were
given by Henry Irving and Ellen Terry.

The early practice of performing *tableaux
vivants* over the New Year was revived some time
after the death of the prince consort. A biblical
tableau of Naomi and Ruth in 1888 was described
by the queen as 'not quite so successful as it
might have been, owing to the ladies getting the
giggles and shaking'.

THE DEATH OF QUEEN VICTORIA

Even in the 1890s Queen Victoria stayed at
Osborne for 90 to 100 days each year, continuing
the daily routine established for over 50 years.
She remained alert, but her eyesight was failing
and Sir Henry Ponsonby was urged to write
larger, and use blacker ink. A combination of
rheumatism and two bad falls meant she was
often pushed in her 'rolling chair'. By 1900 she
was dozing during the day, and failing to sleep at
night. Her first diary entry for 1901 recorded,
'Another year begun & I am feeling so weak &
unwell that I enter upon it sadly.'

On 17 January 1901 the queen suffered a slight
stroke. Members of the family started to arrive
at Osborne, and soon every bed was occupied.
She was nursed in her bedroom, but on 22
January, surrounded by her family, which included
the future Edward VII and Kaiser Wilhelm II of
Germany, the 81-year-old queen of Great Britain
and Ireland, and empress of India died. The duke
of Argyll described the queen's last moments
as 'like a great three-decker ship sinking. She kept
on rallying then sinking'.

The calmness within the Pavilion contrasted with the clamour outside the gates where reporters waited to telegraph the news across the world. Henry Ponsonby's son Frederick (1867–1935) recalled: 'The scene on the hill down to Cowes was disgraceful. Reporters in carriages and on bicycles were seen racing for the post office in East Cowes, and men were shouting as they ran, "The queen is dead"'. It was the end of an era.

Ponsonby described the dining room, where the queen lay in state, which 'was hung round with curtains and draperies. The coffin was covered with crimson velvet and ermine with the crown in diamonds on a cushion, and the Order of the Garter which the Queen had worn on a raised platform covered by the Royal Standard. The room was lighted by eight huge candles and there were palms around the room in addition to the masses of wreaths. It was all gorgeous with colour and most impressive.'

The coffin was guarded by four men from Queen's Company, Grenadier Guards, in scarlet tunics standing with reversed arms, one at each corner, plus a member of the household at the foot of the coffin. On 1 February the coffin,

draped with a white satin pall embroidered by the Royal School of Needlework founded by Princess Helena, with a gold cross in the middle and the royal arms in the corners, was carried from the house by sailors from the royal yacht, and placed on the gun carriage. The whole cortège moved slowly through East Cowes to Trinity Pier where the coffin was placed on the Royal Yacht *Alberta*.

Above: Queen Victoria's coffin lying in state at Osborne, guarded by four Grenadier Guardsmen, 30 January 1901, by Robert Pritchett (1828–1907)

Below: The queen's funeral procession leaves Osborne, 1 February 1901

Above: Princess Beatrice, by Joaquin Sorolla y Bastida, 1908. She was the only one of Queen Victoria's children to retain a home on the Isle of Wight, at Carisbrooke Castle
Right: Naval cadets at the college practising tying knots, c.1905

Facing page: A touching telegram of support sent to George Archer-Shee at Osborne from his father in 1909

The small yacht, accompanied by the *Victoria & Albert* and the *Osborne*, was dwarfed between the battleships and cruisers anchored in two lines all the way to Portsmouth. The queen forbade black for her funeral, and the streets of London were hung with purple, tied with white silk bows. Her coffin, still draped with the white and gold pall, was laid to rest alongside Albert's in the royal mausoleum at Frogmore, Windsor.

OSBORNE IN THE 20TH CENTURY

The death of Queen Victoria at Osborne in 1901 left a vacuum much more dramatic in its consequences for the estate than the death of Albert, its creator. The land and outlying buildings were gradually disposed of.

Osborne was the private possession of the royal family but Edward VII did not need it: Sandringham was more convenient and Barton Manor was enough for overspill accommodation during Cowes Week (Barton was sold in 1922). Only four of his eight siblings were still alive, and Beatrice was the only one to retain a home in the Isle of Wight but she preferred to live in Osborne Cottage. She was also governess of the Isle of Wight and of Carisbrooke Castle, and from 1914 made the governor's residence at Carisbrooke Castle (now English Heritage) her summer home.

The queen bequeathed her private journals to Beatrice, with the injunction that she was to modify portions which she considered unsuitable for preservation. Beatrice copied out an edited version, burning the original volume as each year was completed.

On coronation day 1902 the king wrote: 'As Osborne is sacred to the memory of the late Queen, it is the King's wish that... His People shall always have access to the House which must forever be associated with Her beloved name.' A committee appointed by the king determined in December 1902 that a convalescent home for officers should be established in part of the house, and the stables used for Naval cadets. These principles were enshrined in the 1902 Osborne Estate Act.

The Royal Naval College

The college was established in the grounds in 1903 for the training of officer cadets as a result of reforms leading to a rapid expansion of the Navy. Boys arrived at age 13 and stayed for two years before moving to Britannia Royal Naval College at Dartmouth. Building began in March 1903 to the designs of Henry Nicholas Hawks (1855–1911), architect to the Office of Works, and it was opened by Edward VII the following

August. The first intake was 72, but within two years the number had risen to 400, increasing to its maximum of 500 during the First World War.

The site included classrooms in the former stable block, dormitories (an eventual total of 12), civilian and officers' accommodation (the petty officers' quarters was adapted by English Heritage in 2006 as a reception centre), messing facilities, a training mast, gymnasiums and a cricket pavilion (now used as holiday lets). The new buildings were designed in an Office of Works version of the fashionable municipal Arts and Crafts style.

Both the future Edward VIII and his brother George VI attended as cadets. Their letters home were full of the usual boyish excitement for all that was going on – meeting the explorers Shackleton and Scott, performing in a pantomime,

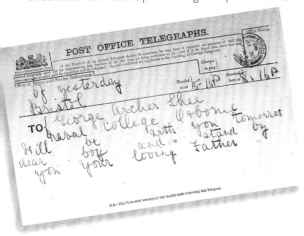

or enthusing about the latest crazes. Today, the college is remembered as the setting of the tragic Archer-Shee scandal of 1909, which was dramatised by Terence Rattigan in his play *The Winslow Boy*. George Archer-Shee, an Osborne cadet, had been accused of stealing a five-shilling postal order, and his parents were asked to withdraw him from the Navy. They appealed, and the case went to court. The cadet was finally vindicated to public jubilation, but the family were financially ruined. Having lost his Naval career, Archer-Shee enlisted in the Army in 1914 and was killed at Ypres, Belgium, within the first month of the war.

The college contributed to strengthening the Navy prior to the First World War, but by 1920 the Navy was over-manned, and the number of cadets at Osborne had fallen to about 50. In 1921 the college closed. In 1933 many of the buildings, such as the dormitories (on the site of the visitors' car park), were demolished.

The Convalescent Home

The Edward VII Convalescent Home for Officers serving in His Majesty's Forces was opened in 1904 within part of the main and household wings. It was run by the house governor, who also managed the royal apartments. Two- and three-room suites were converted into bedrooms and bathrooms by H N Hawks, architect to the Office of Works. Furniture was designed by Rowland Bailey of the Office of Works and made by Maples. The terraces were the preserve of the convalescents, and a nine-hole golf course was laid out for their use.

In the First World War officers were not allowed home to convalesce as it delayed their return to the Front; many were sent to Osborne. The poet and author Robert Graves describes being at Osborne during the First World War, when A A Milne (later author of the Christopher Robin stories) was also a patient. Graves was president of the humorous Royal Albert Society. When he found on the beach a fender with frayed rope resembling hair, he dressed it up with wet clothes and draped it with seaweed before alerting the coastguard to the presence of a dead man on the beach. 'The coastguard stopped a few yards off, and exclaimed, holding his nose: "Pooh, don't he 'alf stink!" ' The hoax was reported in the paper.

No major alterations were made until the late 1980s, when it was effectively transformed into a nursing home. However, escalating costs of patient care prompted its closure in 2000.

When he found on the beach a fender with frayed rope resembling hair, he dressed it up with wet clothes and a boot

Below: Cubitt's 1845 kitchens near the Georgian stables were modernised and used by the convalescent home until the 1950s, when they were converted into a garage

A Maid at Osborne

Domestics were only allowed to go to the kitchen if on an errand for matron, so we didn't get to know the kitchen staff

After leaving school at the age of 15 in 1955, Kathy Barter started work as a 'domestic' in the King Edward VII Convalescent Home for Officers, where she entered a household still run with Victorian discipline.

'Full-time maids were expected to live-in then, in a large dormitory. We did have a small room each, but we shared the bathrooms and toilets. I was the youngest and the 15th housemaid then. There were also six parlourmaids and the governor's maid living in our block. There was also the cooks' and kitchen-maids' dormitory. They didn't mix with us and had their own sitting and dining room.

'Domestics were only allowed to go to the kitchen if on an errand for matron, or sent by the supervisor, so we didn't get to know the kitchen staff well. Also, there was the men's dormitory for the valets, porters and others. Of course that was strictly out of bounds, and they also had their own sitting and dining room. Rules were very strict, and everything was more or less run on military lines.'

From Serving Life at Osborne 1955–2000 *by Kathy Barter*

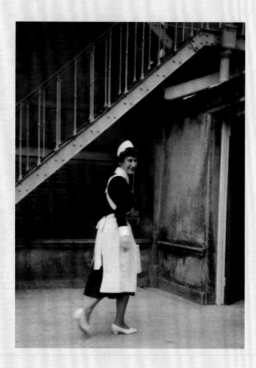

Kathy Barter in the uniform of a parlourmaid, carrying the pig bucket, 1965. 'You were never allowed a dirty apron, or to have your straps twisted'

OSBORNE TODAY

Edward VII did not want the public to have access to Queen Victoria's private rooms in the Pavilion, so the first floor was sealed by iron gates and preserved for over 50 years as a family shrine.

Other apartments were opened to the public free of charge. Carpeting was stripped out during the Edwardian period. Copies were substituted for some paintings, and some major representation schemes were undertaken, notably the rearrangements of the Durbar Room and the Swiss Cottage and museum by Sir Guy Laking during the First World War. Nevertheless, Osborne retains much of its original contents which are part of the Royal Collection. The Office of Works maintained the grounds, but the Victorian planting was abandoned: the terrace parterres were simplified after the last war and in the Swiss Cottage shrubs and flowers replaced vegetables in the children's plots. Osborne's fortunes reached a nadir in the early 1920s, when Victorian art and architecture were out of fashion, but thereafter visitor numbers (who now had to pay) increased.

In 1954 the queen gave permission for the gates to Queen Victoria's private apartments to be unlocked and the public admitted. In 1977, her silver jubilee saw an upsurge in visitor numbers. Some rooms were redecorated, but detailed paint research does not appear to have begun until 1982 when the colour schemes of the Grand Corridor were analysed. Redecoration there was not complete until 1985.

In 1986 English Heritage took over the management of Osborne from the Department of the Environment. In co-operation with the Royal Collection, English Heritage is slowly representing rooms by removing objects which have arrived since 1901 and replacing some which left Osborne earlier. It is seeking to re-emphasize the *raison-d'être* of the house as a family home.

Within the grounds, English Heritage has reinstated Albert's planting and woodland. The conservation of plants and the management of wildlife habitats and ecosystems are significant drivers for modern management of the Osborne estate. Large areas are maintained as wildflower and grass meadows for biodiversity. The estate is also a haven for protected species including red squirrels and pairs of buzzards, which are often seen above the valley from the Swiss Cottage road.